GW00732038

Can

by Iain Gray

Lang**Syne**

PUBLISHING

WRITING *to* REMEMBER

LangSyne

PUBLISHING

WRITING *to* REMEMBER

79 Main Street, Newtongrange,
Midlothian EH22 4NA
Tel: 0131 344 0414   Fax: 0845 075 6085
E-mail: info@lang-syne.co.uk
www.langsyneshop.co.uk

Design by Dorothy Meikle
Printed by Ricoh Print Scotland
© Lang Syne Publishers Ltd 2015

ISBN 978-1-85217-583-2

Campbell

MOTTO:
Forget Not.

CREST:
A boar's head.

NAME variations include:
Cambel
Cambell
Cammell

Chapter one:

The origins of popular surnames

by George Forbes and Iain Gray

If you don't know where you came from, you won't know where you're going is a frequently quoted observation and one that has a particular resonance today when there has been a marked upsurge in interest in genealogy, with increasing numbers of people curious to trace their family roots.

Main sources for genealogical research include census returns and official records of births, marriages and deaths – and the key to unlocking the detail they contain is obviously a family surname, one that has been 'inherited' and passed from generation to generation.

No matter our station in life, we all have a surname – but it was not until about the middle of the fourteenth century that the practice of being identified by a particular surname became commonly established throughout the British Isles.

Previous to this, it was normal for a person to be identified through the use of only a forename.

But as population gradually increased and there were many more people with the same forename, surnames were adopted to distinguish one person, or community, from another.

Many common English surnames are patronymic in origin, meaning they stem from the forename of one's father – with 'Johnson,' for example, indicating 'son of John.'

It was the Normans, in the wake of their eleventh century conquest of Anglo-Saxon England, a pivotal moment in the nation's history, who first brought surnames into usage – although it was a gradual process.

For the Normans, these were names initially based on the title of their estates, local villages and chateaux in France to distinguish and identify these landholdings.

Such grand descriptions also helped enhance the prestige of these warlords and generally glorify their lofty positions high above the humble serfs slaving away below in the pecking order who had only single names, often with Biblical connotations as in Pierre and Jacques.

The only descriptive distinctions among the peasantry concerned their occupations, like 'Pierre the swineherd' or 'Jacques the ferryman.'

Roots of surnames that came into usage in England not only included Norman-French, but also Old French, Old Norse, Old English, Middle English, German, Latin, Greek, Hebrew and the Gaelic languages of the Celts.

The Normans themselves were originally Vikings, or 'Northmen', who raided, colonised and eventually settled down around the French coastline.

The had sailed up the Seine in their longboats in 900AD under their ferocious leader Rollo and ruled the roost in north eastern France before sailing over to conquer England in 1066 under Duke William of Normandy – better known to posterity as William the Conqueror, or King William I of England.

Granted lands in the newly-conquered England, some of their descendants later acquired territories in Wales, Scotland and Ireland – taking not only their own surnames, but also the practice of adopting a surname, with them.

But it was in England where Norman rule and custom first impacted, particularly in relation to the adoption of surnames.

This is reflected in the famous *Domesday Book*, a massive survey of much of England and Wales, ordered by William I, to determine who owned what, what it was worth and therefore how much they were liable to pay in taxes to the voracious Royal Exchequer.

Completed in 1086 and now held in the National Archives in Kew, London, 'Domesday' was an Old English word meaning 'Day of Judgement.'

This was because, in the words of one contemporary chronicler, "its decisions, like those of the Last Judgement, are unalterable."

It had been a requirement of all those English landholders – from the richest to the poorest – that they identify themselves for the purposes of the survey and for future reference by means of a surname.

This is why the *Domesday Book*, although written in Latin as was the practice for several centuries with both civic and ecclesiastical records, is an invaluable source for the early appearance of a wide range of English surnames.

Several of these names were coined in connection with occupations.

These include Baker and Smith, while Cooks, Chamberlains, Constables and Porters were to be found carrying out duties in large medieval households.

The church's influence can be found in names such as Bishop, Friar and Monk while the popular name of Bennett derives from the late fifth to mid-sixth century Saint Benedict, founder of the Benedictine order of monks.

The early medical profession is represented by Barber, while businessmen produced names that include Merchant and Sellers.

Down at the village watermill, the names that cropped up included Millar/Miller, Walker and Fuller, while other self-explanatory trades included Cooper, Tailor, Mason and Wright.

Even the scenery was utilised as in Moor, Hill, Wood and Forrest – while the hunt and the chase supplied names that include Hunter, Falconer, Fowler and Fox.

Colours are also a source of popular surnames, as in Black, Brown, Gray/Grey, Green and White, and would have denoted the colour of the clothing the person habitually wore or, apart from the obvious exception of 'Green', one's hair colouring or even complexion.

The surname Red developed into Reid, while

Blue was rare and no-one wanted to be associated with yellow.

Rather self-important individuals took surnames that include Goodman and Wiseman, while physical attributes crept into surnames such as Small and Little.

Many families proudly boast the heraldic device known as a Coat of Arms, as featured on our front cover.

The central motif of the Coat of Arms would originally have been what was borne on the shield of a warrior to distinguish himself from others on the battlefield.

Not featured on the Coat of Arms, but highlighted on page three, is the family motto and related crest – with the latter frequently different from the central motif.

Adding further variety to the rich cultural heritage that is represented by surnames is the appearance in recent times in lists of the 100 most common names found in England of ones that include Khan, Patel and Singh – names that have proud roots in the vast sub-continent of India.

Echoes of a far distant past can still be found in our surnames and they can be borne with pride in commemoration of our forebears.

Chapter two:

Ancient roots

Although a name particularly identified with Scotland, 'Campbell' is ranked 87th in some lists of the 100 most common surnames found in England today and at 47th in the United Kingdom as a whole.

A family name that boasts Scots-Gaelic roots, it derives from 'cam' and 'beal', indicating 'crooked smile', 'crooked mouth', or 'wry-mouthed', and was originally bestowed as a nickname on someone who either displayed these facial characteristics or who was known for a particularly 'wry', or acerbic turn of phrase.

Although in Scotland the Campbells of today, as Clan Campbell, are identified with Argyll, in the Highlands, before they gained the rugged grandeur that comprises this territory they are thought to have been settled in south-eastern Scotland, which then formed part of a vast swathe of territory known as Bernicia.

Known in Old English as Bernice, or Beornice, Bernicia embraced not only what is now south-eastern Scotland but also what are now the modern-day English counties of Durham and Northumberland.

This may go some way towards explaining why some 'English' bearers of the Campbell name today are particularly identified with these counties.

Referred to in the ninth century *Historia Brittonum*, and described in Old Welsh as *Yr Hen Ogledd – The Old North* – Bernicia was an Anglo-Saxon kingdom that had absorbed kingdoms previously held by ancient Britons such as the Votadini and who included some of those who in much later centuries would come to bear the Campbell name.

This means that flowing through the veins of the Campbells today is a rich and heady mix of bloodlines that include not only those of the Gaels, Celts and the ancient Britons but also that of those Germanic tribes who invaded and settled firstly in the south and east of the island of Britain from about the early fifth century.

Known as the Anglo-Saxons, they were composed of the Jutes, from the area of the Jutland Peninsula in modern Denmark, the Saxons from Lower Saxony, in modern Germany and the Angles from the Angeln area of Germany.

It was the Angles who gave the name 'Engla land', or 'Aengla land' – better known as 'England.'

They held sway in what became England from approximately 550 to 1066, with the main kingdoms those of Sussex, Wessex, Northumbria, Mercia, Kent, East Anglia and Essex.

Whoever controlled the most powerful of these kingdoms was tacitly recognised as overall 'king' – one of the most noted being Alfred the Great, King of Wessex from 871 to 899.

It was during his reign that the famous *Anglo-Saxon Chronicle* was compiled – an invaluable source of Anglo-Saxon history – while Alfred was designated in early documents as *Rex Anglorum Saxonum*, King of the English Saxons.

Other important Anglo-Saxon works include the epic *Beowulf* and the seventh century *Caedmon's Hymn*.

Through the Anglo-Saxons, the language known as Old English developed, later transforming from the eleventh century into Middle English – sources from which many popular English surnames of today derive.

The Anglo-Saxons, meanwhile, had usurped the power of the indigenous Britons such as those who would come to bear the Campbell name and who referred to them as 'Saeson' or 'Saxones.'

It is from this that the Scottish-Gaelic term for 'English people' of 'Sasannach' derives, the Irish Gaelic 'Sasanach' and the Welsh 'Saeson.'

We learn from the *Anglo-Saxon Chronicle* how the religion of the early Anglo-Saxons was one that pre-dated the establishment of Christianity in the British Isles.

Known as a form of Germanic paganism, with roots in Old Norse religion, it shared much in common with the Druidic 'nature-worshipping' religion of the indigenous Britons such as the ancient forebears of the Campbells.

It was in the closing years of the sixth century that Christianity began to take a hold in Britain, while by approximately 690 it had become the 'established' religion of Anglo-Saxon England.

The first serious shock to Anglo-Saxon control came in 789 in the form of sinister black-sailed Viking ships that appeared over the horizon off the island monastery of Lindisfarne, in the northeast of the country.

Lindisfarne was sacked in an orgy of violence and plunder, setting the scene for what would be many more terrifying raids on the coastline of not only England, but also Ireland and Scotland.

But the Vikings, or 'Northmen', in common with the Anglo-Saxons of earlier times, were raiders who eventually stayed – establishing, for example, what became Jorvik, or York, and the trading port of Dublin, in Ireland. Through intermarriage, the bloodlines of the Anglo-Saxons also became infused with that of the Vikings.

But there would be another infusion of the blood of the 'Northmen' in the wake of the Norman Conquest of 1066 – a key event in English history that sounded the death knell of Anglo-Saxon supremacy.

By this date England had become a nation with several powerful competitors to the throne.

In what were extremely complex family, political and military machinations, the king was Harold II, who had succeeded to the throne following the death of Edward the Confessor.

But his right to the throne was contested by two powerful competitors – his brother-in-law King Harold Hardrada of Norway, in alliance with Tostig, Harold II's brother, and Duke William II of Normandy.

In what has become known as The Year of Three Battles, Hardrada invaded England and gained victory over the English king on September 20 at the battle of Fulford, in Yorkshire.

Five days later, however, Harold II decisively defeated his brother-in-law and brother at the battle of Stamford Bridge.

But he had little time to celebrate his victory, having to immediately march south from Yorkshire to encounter a mighty invasion force led by Duke William of Normandy that had landed at Hastings, in East Sussex.

Harold's battle-hardened but exhausted force confronted the Normans on October 14, drawing up a strong defensive position, at the top of Senlac Hill, building a shield wall to repel Duke William's cavalry and infantry.

The Normans suffered heavy losses, but through a combination of the deadly skill of their archers and the ferocious determination of their cavalry they eventually won the day.

Morale had collapsed on the battlefield as word spread through the ranks that Harold, last of the Anglo-Saxon kings, had been killed

William was declared King of England on December 25, and the complete subjugation of his Anglo-Saxon subjects followed.

Those Normans who had fought on his behalf were rewarded with the lands of Anglo-Saxons, while within an astonishingly short space of time, Norman manners, customs and law were imposed on England – laying the basis for what subsequently became established 'English' custom and practice.

The Campbells, meanwhile, came to stamp an indelible mark on the historical record and bearers of the name today throughout the United Kingdom are entitled to share in the proud Scottish Clan Campbell's motto of *Forget Not* and crest of a boar's head.

The 26th chief of all the Campbells and 12th Duke of Argyll was Sir Ian Campbell, Keeper of the Great Seal of Scotland and of the castles of Dunoon, Carrick, Dunstaffnage and Tarbert and also Admiral of the Western Coast.

Born in 1934, he died in 2001, and was succeeded as 13th Duke of Argyll by his son Torquhil Ian Campbell, born in 1968, and who in 2002 married Eleanor M. Cadbury, of the famous Cadbury multi-national confectionery company that was first established in Birmingham in 1824.

Chapter three:

Honours and distinction

In the field of conflict, bearers of the Campbell name have been recipients of the Victoria Cross (VC), the highest award for gallantry in the face of enemy action for British and Commonwealth forces.

Born in 1876, John Vaughan Campbell was an English-born recipient of the honour.

A son of the 2nd Earl of Cawdor, who was killed fighting as a British Army captain in the Zulu War of 1879, he had been a temporary lieutenant-colonel commanding the 3rd Battalion, Coldstream Guards, during the First World War when he performed the actions for which he was awarded the VC.

This was in September of 1916 at Givenchy, France, during the battle of the Somme, when he rallied his men to successfully attack an enemy machine-gun nest that had been wreaking havoc among their ranks.

Later promoted to the rank of Brigadier-General, he died in 1944, while his VC is now on display at the Guards Regimental Headquarters (Coldstream Guards RHQ), in Wellington Barracks, London.

Born in Ayrshire in 1917, Flying Officer Kenneth Campbell was a posthumous recipient of the VC during the Second World War.

This was when, piloting a Bristol Beaufort aircraft over Brest harbour, France, with great precision he managed to launch a torpedo that caused extensive damage to the mighty German battlecruiser *Gneisenau* – damage that resulted in the cruiser being put out of action for six vital months.

Campbell and his three crew mates were killed when their aircraft was hit by enemy fire and crashed into the harbour while, in recognition of their daring and skilled attack, the Germans recovered their bodies and buried them with full military honours.

From warfare to the world of business, one particularly enterprising bearer of the Campbell name and one whose legacy survives to this day in the form of a popular range of foodstuffs, was Joseph Albert Campbell, the founder along with Abraham Anderson in 1869 of the *Campbell's Soup Company*.

Born in 1817 in Bridgeton, New Jersey, he had been a fruit merchant when he formed what proved to be his highly successful partnership with Anderson, an icebox manufacturer.

Producing a range of soups, condiments,

minced meats, jellies and canned vegetables, the company rapidly flourished and, after Anderson left the partnership in 1876, became the *Joseph A. Campbell Preserve Company*.

Joseph A. Campbell died in 1900, while the company now also produces a range of health beverages and snacks.

Known now as the *Campbell Soup Company*, or *Campbell's*, and headquartered in Camden, New Jersey, an iconic silkscreen image of a can of Campbell's soup – *Small Torn Campbell Soup Can (Pepper Pot)* – executed by the late New York-based 'pop' artist Andy Warhol in 1962, fetched $11.8m at auction in 2006.

In the world of politics, Alastair Campbell, born in 1957 in Keighley, West Riding of Yorkshire, and the son of a Scottish veterinary surgeon, is the journalist, author and broadcaster who served from 1997 to 2003 as director of strategy and communications for British Prime Minister Tony Blair.

It was in his role of main political aide to Tony Blair that in the run-up to the invasion of Iraq in 2003 he became embroiled in controversy over allegations that he had been involved in 'sexing-up', or distorting, intelligence information concerning weapons of mass destruction held by Iraq and to justify the invasion of the country.

Selected extracts from the voluminous diaries that he compiled during his years serving Blair were first published in 2007 as *The Blair Years*.

Not only a veteran British politician but also a former record-holding athlete, Sir Walter Menzies Campbell was born in Glasgow in 1941.

Better known as Ming Campbell, he served as leader of the Liberal Democrats from March of 2006 until October of 2007 while, as an athlete, it was from 1967 until 1974 that he held the British record for the 100-metres sprint.

Member of Parliament for North East Fife and a spokesperson for his party on foreign affairs, he was prominent in his opposition to the invasion of Iraq.

In Canadian politics, Avril Phaedra Douglas Campbell, better known as Kim Campbell, is the politician who, as leader of the Progressive Conservative Party, served as 19th Prime Minister of Canada from June of 1993 until November of the same year.

Born in 1947 in Port Alberni, British Columbia, the politician, diplomat, writer and university professor is the first and, to date, the only female Prime Minister of Canada.

Having also served as a Justice Minister, it was during her tenure in this post that she was responsible for the passing of legislation known as the Rape Shield Law that protects an alleged victim's sexual past from being exploited during a trial.

One of the most poignant tales concerning bearers of the Campbell name relates to Mary Campbell, fondly known as Highland Mary, and who was immortalised in verse by the great Scottish bard Robert Burns.

Born in 1763 at Dunoon, on the west coast of Scotland, it was while working as a young lass on a farm near Tarbolton, in Burns' native Ayrshire, that Mary is first thought to have met the bard.

Burns penned the famous poems *The Highland Lassie O*, *Highland Mary* and, after her untimely death from typhoid at the age of 23, *To Mary in Heaven*.

It is thought that, shortly before her death and Burns' later marriage to Jean Armour, the poet had hoped to emigrate from Scotland to Jamaica with Mary, after the couple had already plighted their undying 'troth' or love for one another in an old and informal Scottish marriage ceremony that involved exchanging Bibles over a river.

Highland Mary

Ye banks, and braes, and streams around
The castle o' Montgomery,
Green be your woods, and fair your flowers,
Your waters never drumlie!
There Simmer first unfald her robes,
And there the langest tarry:
For there I took the last Fareweel
O' my sweet Highland Mary.

How sweetly bloom'd the gay, green birk,
How rich the hawthorn's blossom;
As underneath their fragrant shade,
I clasp'd her to my bosom!
The golden Hours, on angel wings,
Flew o'er me and my Dearie;
For dear to me as light and life
Was my sweet Highland Mary.

Wi' mony a vow, and lock'd embrace,
Our parting was fu' tender;
And pledging aft to meet again,
We tore oursels asunder:
But Oh! fell Death's untimely frost,
That nipt my Flower sae early!
Now green's the sod, and cauld's the clay,
That wraps my Highland Mary!

O pale, pale now, those rosy lips,
I aft hae kiss'd sae fondly!
And clos'd for ay the sparkling glance,
That dwalt on me sae kindly!
And mouldering now in silent dust,
That heart that lo'ed me dearly!
But still within my bosom's core
Shall live my Highland Mary.

Chapter four:

On the world stage

A multi-award-winning country music singer, guitarist and actor, Glen Campbell was born Glen Travis Campbell in 1936 in the small community of Billstown, in Pike County, Arkansas.

Of Scottish roots through his father and one of twelve children, he first picked up the guitar as a young lad and was taught to play by one of his uncles.

When aged 18, Campbell joined his uncle's band – Dick Bills and the Sandia Mountain Boys – and soon began to also star in radio shows.

Having honed his skills on the guitar, he became a highly sought after session musician and part of a group of studio musicians known as The Wrecking Crew – playing on recordings by other artistes and bands ranging from Bobby Darin, Frank Sinatra and Nat King Cole to Elvis Presley, the Beach Boys and The Monkees.

As an artiste in his own right, he has enjoyed international success with hits that include *Gentle on My Mind*, *Wichita Lineman*, *Rhinestone Cowboy*, *Galveston* and *Southern Nights*, while his many awards include the Country Music Association (CMA) award in 1968 for Entertainer of the Year.

As an actor, his role in the 1969 film *True Grit*, starring beside John Wayne, won him a Golden Globe nomination for Most Promising Actor, while in the 1960s and 1970s he also hosted the popular *The Glen Campbell Goodtime Hour* on American television.

Recognised as having played a prominent role in the British folk music revival of the 1960s, **Ian Campbell** was the folk musician born in Aberdeen in 1933.

Moving from Scotland as a teenager to work as an engraver in Birmingham's Jewellery Quarter, he joined the choir of a local branch of the Workers' Music Association and, in 1957, formed the Clarion Skiffle Group, later known as the Ian Campbell Folk Group, and whose 1962 *Ceilidh at the Crown* was the first live folk music recording to be released on vinyl.

Later working as an editor and television presenter for TV-am and also as a community arts worker in the Dudley area of Birmingham, he died in 2012.

Continuing a musical tradition, his sons **Alistair Ian "Ali" Campbell**, **Robin Campbell** and

Duncan Campbell have all been members of the band UB40, whose best-selling hits include *Red, Red Wine*.

On American shores, Michael Wayne Campbell, better known as **Mike Campbell**, is the guitarist, songwriter and record producer born in 1950 in Florida.

Known for his work with the band Tom Petty and the Heartbreakers, he has also produced the Tom Petty solo albums *Full Moon Fever*, *Highway Companion* and *Wallflowers*.

Back on British shores, Philip Campbell, better known as **Wizzo Campbell**, is the Welsh musician, born in 1961, who since 1984 has been lead guitarist of the heavy metal band Motörhead.

From music to the stage, **Julia Campbell**, born in 1962 in Huntsville, Alabama, is the American actress whose film credits include *Romy and Michele's High School Reunion* and the 2006 *Tillamook Treasure*, while television credits include *Ally McBeal*, *The Mentalist* and *The Shield*.

Born in 1937 in Twickenham, **Colin Campbell** is the English actor whose big screen credits include the 1963 *The Leather Boys*, the 1964 *Saturday Night Out* and, from 1990, *Nuns on the Run*.

Born in 1961 in Edinburgh and adopted when he was four days' old, Nicholas Andrew Argyll Campbell is the Scottish radio and television presenter and journalist better known as **Nicky Campbell**.

Having presented television programmes that include *Wheel of Fortune*, *Watchdog* and *Long Lost Family*, and hosting *Top of the Pops* for a time, he is also known as a presenter of BBC Radio 5 Live's breakfast programme.

On Australian shores, **Tim Campbell**, born in Sydney in 1975, is the actor best known for his role of Dan Baker in the television soap *Home and Away*.

Behind the camera lens, **David E. Campbell** is the American sound engineer who won an Academy Award for Best Sound for the 1999 film *The Matrix* and was also the recipient of nominations for other films that include the 2000 *The Perfect Storm*, the 2003 *Pirates of the Caribbean: The Curse of the Black Pearl* and, from 2006, *Flags of Our Fathers*.

Born in Detroit in 1930, **Charles L. Campbell** was the American sound engineer who won Academy Awards for Best Sound Editing for the 1983 *E.T. the Extra-Terrestrial*, the 1986 *Back to the Future* and the 1989 *Who Framed Roger Rabbit*.

The recipient in 2001 of the Career Achievement Award from the Motion Pictures Sound Editors and having served for a time as governor of the Academy of Motion Picture Arts and Sciences (AMPAS), he died in 2013.

On the catwalk, **Naomi Campbell**, born in 1970 in Streatham, London, of mixed African-Jamaican and Chinese descent, is the English supermodel whose first taste of fame came when she was aged only seven in the music video for Jamaican reggae star Bob Marley's *Is This Love*.

Having modelled for fashion houses that include Gianni Versace, her personal life has also hit the media headlines through a number of convictions for assault and her reported relationships with other celebrities who include the boxer Mike Tyson and the American actor Robert De Niro.

Bearers of the Campbell name have also excelled in the highly competitive world of sport.

On the fields of European football, Sulzeer Jeremiah Campbell, born in Plaistow, Newham, London in 1974 to Jamaican parents, is the English retired footballer better known as **Sol Campbell**.

Making his debut as a professional footballer when aged 18 with Tottenham Hotspur, the talented central defender also played for other clubs that include Arsenal, Portsmouth and Notts County, while he played for England in three World Cups – in 1998, 2002 and 2006.

Captain of the England team in 1998, this made him what was then the youngest player to hold the honour since the late Bobby Moore.

Nicknamed "The White Pele" and "The Pele of the North", in recognition of his skills with the ball that rivalled those of the legendary Brazilian footballer of the name, **George Campbell** is the Scottish former professional player born in 1957 in the small Scottish Highland town of Caol, near Fort William.

One of only three players to have made their debut aged just 16 for Scottish club Aberdeen – with whom the midfielder won the 1976 final of the Scottish League Cup against Celtic – he also played for a time with Australian club South Melbourne.

From football to the athletics track, **Darren Campbell** is the record-holding English former sprint athlete born in 1973 in Moss Side, Manchester.

A competitor in both the 100-metres and 200-metres sprint events in addition to the 4x100-metres relay, he became the European record holder in the latter event with a time of 37.73 seconds at the 1998 Commonwealth Games.

The recipient of medals that include silver in the 200-metres event at the 2000 Olympics and also honoured with an MBE, he has also worked with a number of English Premier League football clubs to improve players' sprinting ability.

In the swimming pool, **Catie Campbell** and her younger sister **Bronte Campbell** – born respectively in 1992 and 1994 – are the Australian swimmers who in 2014 became the first sisters to take gold and silver medals after competing in the same event.

This was in the 100-metres event at the Commonwealth Games in Glasgow, where Catie won the gold medal and her sister the silver.

On the golf course, **Michael Campbell**, born in 1969 in Hawari, Taranki, is the New Zealand golfer of Maori and Scottish descent who in 2005 won both the U.S. Open and the HSBC World Play Championship.

One particularly intrepid bearer of the Campbell name and one gifted with an incredible amount of stamina is **Ffyona Campbell**, the British long-distance runner who, after a gruelling period that spanned eleven years, became the first woman to walk around the world.

Born in 1967 in Totnes, Devon, it was in 1983, when she was aged 16, that she walked over a period of 49 days from John o' Groats on the extreme northern tip of the Scottish mainland to Land's End on the southern tip of the English mainland.

Two years later, she crossed the United States from New York to Los Angeles, while other parts of her marathon world trek saw her walking 3,200 miles from Sydney to Perth, in Australia, in 95 days and later 9,000 miles across the length of Africa from Cape Town, South Africa, to Tangiers, Morocco.

In 1994, supporting a range of charities along the way through sponsorship, she walked through Europe – through Spain and then France – finally completing her exhausting trek by walking from Dover and back to John o' Groats, arriving there on October 14, 1994.

Her experiences, that included at times having to walk through African war zones, are detailed in three of her books that include *On Foot Through Africa*.

One particularly famous father and son bearers of the proud name of Campbell were the daring English world speed record holders on land and water **Malcolm Campbell** and **Donald Campbell**.

Born in 1885, Malcolm Campbell, later ennobled as Sir Malcolm Campbell, established a world land speed record of 301 mph in 1935 and, four years later, a water-speed record of 141.7 mph.

He died in 1948, while his son Donald, born in 1921 at Canbury House, Kingston upon Thames, Surrey, broke eight world speed records in the 1950s and 1960s.

He set world speed-water records in the jet-powered *Bluebird K7* hydroplane between July of 1955 and December of 1964 – the first being achieved at Ullswater, in the English Lake District, when he recorded a speed of 202.32 mph.

Tragedy struck when, on January 4, 1967, at Lake Coniston in the Lake District, Campbell was killed while attempting to attain a new speed record of 300 mph.

At immensely high speed, *Bluebird K7* disastrously cartwheeled across the water and broke up, and while Campbell's mascot of his teddy bear *Mr Whoppit* was recovered at the time, it was not until May of 2001 that his body was recovered –

seven months after the first sections of the wrecked *Bluebird K7* were located by divers.

Donald Campbell was portrayed by the actor Anthony Hopkins in the 1988 BBC television film *Across the Lake*, while his father was portrayed by Robert Hardy in the 1979 BBC television drama *Speed King*.

In 2003, meanwhile, in the television film *Campbell at Coniston*, the BBC utilised colour film that had been taken in the weeks leading up to the tragedy by John Lomax, an amateur filmmaker from the Lake District.